HUDSON TAYLOR
on
SPIRITUAL SECRETS

A 30-DAY DEVOTIONAL TREASURY

Compiled and Edited by
LANCE WUBBELS

Emerald Books

P.O. Box 635
Lynnwood, WA 98046

OTHER CHRISTIAN LIVING CLASSICS

30-DAY DEVOTIONAL TREASURIES

Charles Finney on Spiritual Power
George Müller on Faith
Andrew Murray on Holiness
Hudson Taylor on Spiritual Secrets
Charles Spurgeon on Prayer
R. A. Torrey on the Holy Spirit

CHARLES SPURGEON: BELIEVER'S LIFE SERIES

Grace Abounding in a Believer's Life
A Passion for Holiness in a Believer's Life
The Power of Prayer in a Believer's Life
Spiritual Warfare in a Believer's Life
The Triumph of Faith in a Believer's Life
What the Holy Spirit Does in a Believer's Life

CHARLES SPURGEON: LIFE OF CHRIST SERIES

The Power of Christ's Miracles
The Power of Christ's Prayer Life
The Power of Christ's Second Coming
The Power of Christ's Tears
The Power of Christ the Warrior
The Power of the Cross of Christ

F. B. MEYER: BIBLE CHARACTER SERIES

The Life of Abraham: The Obedience of Faith
The Life of David: Shepherd, Psalmist, King
The Life of Joseph: Beloved, Hated, Exalted
The Life of Moses: The Servant of God
The Life of Paul: A Servant of Jesus Christ
The Life of Peter: Fisherman, Disciple, Apostle

Hudson Taylor on Spiritual Secrets
Copyright © 1998 by Lance Wubbels

Published by Emerald Books
P.O. Box 635
Lynnwood, WA 98046

ISBN 1-883002-45-1

Printed in the United States of America.

INTRODUCTION

James Hudson Taylor (1832–1905) was born in Yorkshire, England, and experienced a deep conversion to Christ at the age of seventeen. He soon felt a strong call to the almost closed empire of China and landed at Shanghai in 1854 as an agent of the short-lived Chinese Evangelization Society. Problems at the mission's home base threw him back on faith and prayer for his support, and a succession of providences caused him to sever connections with the Society. He made several evangelistic forays into the closed interior and adopted Chinese dress. In 1858 he married Maria Dyer despite the opposition of other missionaries who considered him a "poor, unconnected nobody."

Invalided back to England in 1860, he carried a burden for inland China and the millions without Christ. When the empire opened to Westerners, he could find no mission willing to send him, so he founded the inter-denominational China Inland Mission (CIM) in 1865, asking God to send "24 willing, skillful laborers," two for each unreached province. They sailed in 1866. His wife, Maria, died four years later.

Despite persecution, opposition from missionaries, and difficulties of culture and language, the CIM established itself as the "shock troops" of Protestant advance. Taylor's burden was to bring the Gospel to every creature, and by 1895 he led 641 missionaries, about half the entire Protestant force in China. Few men have been such an instrument in God's hands for proclaiming the gospel to a vast population and bringing so many Christian churches into being. His great spiritual qualities and the caliber of the CIM, together with his writings and world travels, gave him an influence far beyond China and led to similar faith-missions being founded. Taylor died at Changsha in the heart of inland China, thus crowning a life of Christlike devotion and undaunted witness to which it is difficult to find many parallels.

Lance Wubbels, compiler and editor

WORKING WITH GOD

—⟨∞⟩—

Do not be anxious about anything, but in everything,
by prayer and petition, with thanksgiving, present
your requests to God.
—Philippians 4:6

I cannot stress enough the importance of understanding this principle of working with God, and of asking Him for everything. If the work we do is at the command of God, then we can go to Him with full confidence for the workers we need. And when God gives the workers, *then* we can go to Him for the means. Our mission always accepts a suitable worker, whether we have the funds or not. Then we say, "Dear friend, your first work will be to join with us in praying for the money to send you to China." As soon as there is money enough, the time of the year and the circumstances being suitable, the friend goes out. We do not wait until there is a remittance in hand to give him when he gets there. The Lord will provide that.

Our Father is a very experienced One: He knows very well that His children wake up with a good appetite every morning, and He always provides breakfast for them. "His bread will be supplied, and water will not fail him" (Isa. 33:16). He sustained three million Israelites in the wilderness for forty years. We do not expect that He will send three million missionaries to China, but if He did, He would have plenty of means to sustain them all. Let us see that we keep God before our eyes, that we walk in His ways and seek to please and glorify Him in everything we do. Depend upon it: *God's work done in God's way will never lack God's supplies.*

When the supplies do not come in, it is time to ask, What's wrong? It may be only a temporary trial of faith; but if there is faith, it will bear the trying, and if not it is well that we should not be deceived. It is very easy, with money in the pocket and food in the cupboard to think you have faith in God. Frances Havergal said: "Those who trust Him wholly find Him wholly true." But my experience proves that to those who do not trust Him wholly, He does not break His word: "If we are faithless, he will remain faithful, for he cannot disown himself" (2 Tim. 2:13).

—————

Father, how easy it is to assume that our faith is strong and healthy, when in fact our faith lies dormant and our lives remain unchallenged to believe You for great things. Challenge my faith with a new sense of what You want me to trust You for. Amen.

who are not really in Christ at all. The subject of this chapter in not salvation, but fruitfulness. The unfruitful branch taken away does not mean a soul lost, but a life lost. Men may be saved so as by fire, saved as Lot was saved out of Sodom—property gone, wife and children gone—saved, with a loss the extent of which eternity alone will reveal. The Lord keep His people from loving the world or the things of the world.

Not only does the great Gardener remove the fruitless branches but He prunes the fruitful ones, that they may bring forth more fruit. The word rendered "prune" is the verbal form of that rendered "clean" in the next verse. The methods of the divine Gardener are not necessarily severe. He cleanses by the application of the Word; and where the gentle voice of the Spirit through the Word is listened to, severe and painful discipline may be unneeded. How much of restraint as well as of constraint we might be spared, did the Word of God dwell in us more richly, and were the leadings of the Spirit more implicitly obeyed!

—∿∿—

Divine Gardener, I confess that the pruning and the cleaning that You are doing in my life is good. Help me always to see that it is Your hand at work—not chance or fate. Apply the power of Your Word into my life that I might bear more fruit. Amen.

THE SOURCE OF POWER

—∿∿—

One thing God has spoken, two things have I heard: that you, O God, are strong, and that you, O Lord, are loving.
—Psalm 62:11–12

God Himself is the great source of power. It is His possession. "You, O God, are strong," and He manifests it according to His sovereign will. Yet not in an erratic or arbitrary manner, but according to His declared purpose and promises. True, our opponents and hindrances are many and mighty, but our God, the living God, is Almighty.

God tells us by His prophet Daniel that the people who know their God shall be strong and do exploits, resisting the evil one. While it is generally true that knowledge is power, it is supremely true in the case of the knowledge of God. Those who know their God do not *attempt* to do exploits, but *do* them. Search the Scriptures in vain to find any command to *attempt* to do anything. God's commands are always "Do this." If the command is from God, our only course is to obey.

Further, God's power is available power. We are supernatural people, born again by a supernatural birth, kept by a supernatural power, sustained on supernatural food, taught by a supernatural Teacher from a supernatural Book. We are led by a supernatural Captain in right paths to assured victories. The risen Savior, before He ascended on high, said, "All authority in heaven and on earth has been given to me. Therefore go and make disciples" (Matt. 28:18–19).

He also said to His disciples, "You will receive power when the Holy Spirit comes on you" (Acts 1:8). Not many days after this, in answer to united and continued prayer, the Holy Spirit did come upon them, and they were all filled. Praise God, He remains with us still. The power given is not a gift from the Holy Spirit. He Himself is the power. Today He is as truly available and as mighty in power as He was on the day of Pentecost. But since the days of Pentecost, has the whole church ever put aside every other work and waited upon Him for ten days, that that power might be manifested? We give too much attention to method and machinery and resources, and too little to the source of power.

———

Blessed Jesus, who redeemed Your people with Your own heart's blood, will You not with more of Your own Spirit baptize Your people, that others who are perishing for lack of knowledge may also be fed with living manna and have the light of life. Amen.

THE DIVINE GARDENER

———

"He cuts off every branch in me that bears no fruit, while every branch that does bear fruit he prunes so that it will be even more fruitful."
—John 15:2

To no apprentice hand is committed the culture of the true Vine; the great Father Himself undertakes this alone. Speaking of Christ's people as a flock, under-shepherds are found, but as a branch each believer is directly united to the true Vine, that receives all things needful through the care of the great Gardener Himself. This is very blessed; over-pruning or under-pruning is impossible. He will train and sustain every individual branch; the needs of each are known to Him and He will supply sunshine or shade, darkness or light, fair weather or shower, as seems best to Him. The branch may abide satisfied without care or worry.

We learn from these solemn words that it is possible to be in Christ and yet to bear no fruit. These words do not refer to mere professors,

FAITH

———<small>⁓⁓⁓</small>———

"Have faith in God," Jesus answered.
—Mark 11:22

Hold God's faithfulness. Abraham held God's faith, and offered up Isaac, believing that God was able to raise him up. Moses held God's faith, and led the millions of Israel into the howling wilderness. Joshua knew Israel well and was not ignorant of the fortifications of the Canaanites or of their military prowess, but he held God's faithfulness and led Israel across the Jordan. The apostles held God's faith, and were undaunted by the hatred of the Jews or by the hostility of the heathen. And what shall I say more, for the time would fail me to tell of those "who through faith conquered kingdoms, administered justice, and gained what was promised; who shut the mouths of lions, quenched the fury of the flames, and escaped the edge of the sword; whose weakness was turned to strength; and who became powerful in battle and routed foreign armies" (Heb. 11:33–34).

Satan, too, has his creed: "Doubt God's faithfulness." "Has God said? Are you not mistaken as to His commands? He could not really mean that. You are taking an extreme view. You take the meaning of the words too literally." Ah! How constantly, and alas, how successfully, are such arguments used to prevent wholehearted trust in God, wholehearted consecration to God.

All God's giants have been weak men, who did great things for God because they believed that God would be with them. See the cases of David, of Jonathan and his armor-bearer, of Asa, Jehoshaphat, and many others. Oh, if there is a living God, faithful and true, let us hold His faithfulness. Holding His faithfulness, we may go into every province in China, no matter how dark. Holding His faithfulness, we may face, with calm and sober but confident assurance of victory, every difficulty and danger. We may count on grace for the work, on financial aid, on needful facilities, and on ultimate success. Let us not give Him a partial trust, but daily, hourly, serve Him, as we "have faith in God."

———*∾∾∾*———

Almighty God, I desire to hold Your faithfulness, regardless of the cost to me or how others will view me. I count upon You to provide all that I need to follow Your every command. Amen.

GOD'S BETTER ANSWER

———⁓⁓⁓———

*"My grace is sufficient for you, for my power
is made perfect in weakness."*
—2 Corinthians 12:9

From both the life of the Lord Jesus and of the apostle Paul, we are given a great deal of light on the question so often asked: "Does God *always* answer prayer?" There are, of course, many prayers that He does not answer—prayers that are asked incorrectly, that are contrary to God's revealed will, or those that are not mixed with faith. But there are many other prayers that are proper petitions, offered in a proper spirit, in which nevertheless the answer does not come just in the way in which the offerer may have expected. When a great need is brought before God in prayer, He may answer that prayer by supplying the need or by removing it, just as we may balance a pair of scales by adding to the light scale, or reducing the weight in the other. Paul was distressed by a burden that he did not have the strength to bear, and asked that the burden might be removed. God answered the prayer, not by taking it away, but by showing him the power and the grace to bear it joyfully. Thus that which had been the cause of sorrow and regret now became the occasion of rejoicing and triumph.

And wasn't this really a *better* answer to Paul's prayer than the mere removing of the thorn? The latter course would have left him open to the same trouble when the next distress came, but God's method at once and forever delivered him from *all* the oppression of the present and of all future similar trials. Hence he triumphantly exclaims, "Therefore I will boast all the more gladly about my weaknesses, so that Christ's power may rest on me" (2 Cor. 12:9). Ah! Who would not wish to share in the apostle's thorn in the flesh, if thereby he might be brought in reality into the experience of his deliverance from the oppression of all weakness, all injury, all necessity, all persecutions, all distress; and might know that the very hour and time of weakness was the hour and time of truest strength? Let none fear then to step out in glad obedience to the Master's commands.

—⁓⁓⁓—

Father, You know best how to answer my prayers. Help me to listen for those times when Your answer is to give me the grace to triumph through the problem. I rejoice in the power that comes from Jesus to strengthen my inner life. Amen.

TRUE PROSPERITY

———∾∾∾———

Blessed is the man who does not walk in the
counsel of the wicked or stand in the way
of sinners or sit in the seat of mockers.
—Psalm 1:1

The way of the sinner no more suits a true believer than the way of the believer suits the sinner. As a witness for his Master in the hope of saving the lost, he may go to them, but he will not, like Lot, set his tent toward Sodom. Ah, how many parents who have fluttered moth-like near a flame of sin have seen their children destroyed by it, while they themselves have not escaped unscathed. And how many churches and Christian institutions in the attempt to attract unbelievers by worldly amusements and compromising their values have themselves forfeited the blessing of God, and have so lost spiritual power that those whom they have attracted have not been benefited. Instead of seeing the unregenerate brought to life, a state of indolence and death has crept over themselves. There is no need of, nor room for, any other attraction than that which Christ Himself gave when He said, "But I, when I am lifted up from the earth, will draw all men to myself" (John 12:32). Our Master was always separate from sinners, and the Holy Spirit unmistakably says, "For what do righteousness and wickedness have in common? Or what fellowship can light have with darkness?" (2 Cor. 6:14).

"Or sit in the seat of mockers." The seat of the mocker is one of special danger in this age. Pride, presumption, and scorn are closely linked together, and are far indeed from the mind that is in Christ Jesus. This spirit often shows itself in the present day in the form of irreverent criticism; those who are least qualified for it are found sitting in the seat of judgment rather than taking the place of the inquirer and learner. The Bereans of old did not scornfully reject what seemed to them strange teachings of the apostle Paul, but searched the Scriptures daily to see whether these things were so (Acts 17:11). Now, even the Scriptures themselves are called into question, and the very foundations of the Christian faith are abandoned by men who would be looked upon as apostles of modern thought.

Heavenly Father, everywhere I look, wickedness and sin abound. And in my life, it's easy to sit in the mocker's seat and criticize and scorn other believers and spiritual matters I don't understand. I need Your help to not walk in the way of sin. Help me today. Amen.

"COME" AND "GO"

———∞———

*"Come to me, all you who are weary and
burdened, and I will give you rest."*
—Matthew 11:28

To every toiling, heavy-laden sinner, Jesus
says, "Come to me…and…rest." But there are
many toiling, heavy-laden believers, too. For
them this same invitation is meant. Note well
the words of Jesus, if you are heavy-laden with

with the words: "Whoever is thirsty, let him come; and whoever wishes, let him take the free gift of the water of life" (Rev. 22:17).

How many of the Lord's redeemed people have spent hours, and days, or even months, in sorrow and self-reproach from some imagined duty that they did not have the courage or strength to perform, heavy-laden all the time! How many can tell of the pressure they have felt to speak to another person about his soul, but could not. And how many have done *far worse:* have spoken when they had no message from God, and have done harm rather than good. Oh, how different it would have been had they but first come to Jesus; found rest and living water; and then, when the waters were welling up within, the rivers would have flowed naturally and irrepressibly, and the happy countenance would have said more than the heartfelt words were uttering! No one would then have looked at the face of the speaker and *felt,* "What a dreadful religion his must be!"

THRESHING MOUNTAINS

———⟨∾∾⟩———

*Then Jesus answered, "Woman, you have
great faith! Your request is granted."*
—Matthew 15:28

By faith the Canaanite woman's daughter
was healed, even though she was an unlikely
candidate. By faith the walls of Jericho fell
down—yet what more unlikely! We walk by
faith. Do we? What record is there on high of
things that by faith we have obtained? Is each
step each day an act of faith? Do we, as children of God, really believe the Bible? Are we
ready to take the place of even a worm, as our
Master did: "But I am a worm and not a man"
(Ps. 22:6). Or if we realize our powerlessness
and our insignificance, do we believe that it is
possible—that it is God's will for us—that we
should thresh mountains? "Do not be afraid, O
worm Jacob," said the Lord by the prophet of
old, "I will make you into a threshing sledge,
new and sharp, with many teeth. You will
thresh the mountains and crush them, and

reduce the hills to chaff. You will winnow them, the wind will pick them up, and a gale will blow them away. But you will rejoice in the LORD and glory in the Holy One of Israel" (Isa. 41:14–16).

How then, do we ask, are we to thresh mountains? Let us listen to our Master: "Have faith in God. I tell you the truth, if anyone says to this mountain, 'Go, throw yourself into the sea,' and does not doubt in his heart but believes that what he says will happen, it will be done for him" (Mark 11:22–23). Do you ask when this shall be? The Lord continues in the following verse (vs. 24): "Whatever you ask for in prayer, believe that you have received it, and it will be yours." Let us therefore "not be anxious about anything, but in everything, by prayer and petition, with thanksgiving, present your requests to God" (Phil. 4:6).

Now let us stop and ask ourselves: what do we desire? And then let us claim the promise at once. Have we unsaved loved ones? Have we difficulties to conquer? Have we mountains to remove? Then let us take it to the Lord in prayer.

———*◦◦◦*———

Father, there are mountains that need threshing in my life. By faith in Your unmerited favor and grace, I take hold of You and Your promises. Be great in my life today. Amen.

THE BLESSING OF GIVING

———∞∞∞———

"In everything I did, I showed you that by this kind of hard work we must help the weak, remembering the words the Lord Jesus himself said: 'It is more blessed to give than to receive.'"

—Acts 20:35

Oh, that my pen may be anointed as with fresh oil, while I seek to bring my own soul, and the soul of my readers, more fully under the influence of this truth!

Our gracious Lord did not content Himself with merely giving utterance to this truth; He embodied it in life. He exhibited it in death. He emptied Himself that we might be filled. He gave—ah! What did He not give?— He gave Himself for us. Oh, for hearts to apprehend and live this out!

Why is our fullness in Christ so little experienced? Why is it not enjoyed more? Simply because we fail to give freely. How little does the Church realize how she is *impoverishing* herself, while she is to an awfully large extent leaving the world to perish through her unbelief, her selfishness, her miserliness. What does her life say to the world? Christ has give her light; she denies it to the perishing. Christ has said, "to *every* creature"; the Church says, "No, no, no! At home to some extent, if you like, but abroad—No. A few missionaries, if you like, but many—No. Will I impoverish myself for the sake of the perishing? Never."

We rejoice to know that there are many who believe that it *is* more blessed to give than to receive; but we unhesitatingly affirm that the general testimony given by the professing Church, as a whole, to the unbelieving world at large is that it is *not* more blessed to give than to receive. No wonder skepticism increases and unbelief prospers!

Whether we believe it or not, "it is more blessed to give than to receive." If we will become givers, He will minister to us both seed for our sowing and bread for our eating, and we shall always have all sufficiency in all things and abound in all good works. Only become givers, and it is immaterial whether you have five loaves or five hundred; the larger number would no more suffice, apart from divine and multiplying power, than the smaller.

———∽∾∿∽———

Jesus, You gave up everything that I might have eternal life. Have I held back in my giving to You? Touch the world through my life as I reach out to serve others. Amen.

THE BLESSING OF THE FATHER

—◦◦◦—

*"The LORD bless you and keep you; the LORD
make his face shine upon you and be
gracious to you; the LORD turn his face
toward you and give you peace."*
—Numbers 6:24–26

In the light of the fuller revelation of the New Testament we can hardly fail to see in this threefold benediction the blessing of the Father, of the Son, and of the Holy Spirit. Viewed in this light, we see in the words fuller beauty and appropriateness. Let us take the first clause, then, as the Father's blessing.

Considered as a father's blessing, could anything be more appropriate than "The LORD bless you and keep you"? Is it not just what every loving father seeks to do—to bless and keep his children? He does not find it an unwelcome task, but his greatest delight. Offer to relieve him of the responsibility and to adopt his child, and see what his reply will be! Nor may we confine ourselves to paternal love alone, but take it as embracing the love of the mother as well,"for this is what the LORD says:....As a mother comforts her child, so will I comfort you" (Isa. 66:12–13). And we all know how the mother-love delights to lavish itself on the objects of its care. With a patience that never tires, and an endurance almost inexhaustible, and a care all but unlimited, how often has the mother sacrificed her very life for her babe? But strong as is a mother's love, it may fail; God's love never.

It was one of the objects of our Savior's mission to reveal to us that, in Christ Jesus, God is our Father. How He delighted to bring out this precious truth the Sermon on the Mount bears witness.

And what a glorious Father He is!—the source of all true fatherhood and mother-hood. The sum of all human goodness, and tenderness, and love is but as the dewdrop to the sun. How safe too! Often when the love of earthly parents has not failed, yet have they been powerless to bless and keep. And it is an individual blessing: "The LORD bless *you* and keep *you*," including every form of blessing, temporal as well as spiritual.

———

Heavenly Father, what a joy it is to be Your child! Your love and care and keeping power surrounds me. May I love You today and bless You as You bless me. Amen.

THE BLESSING OF THE SON

—〰〰〰—

"The LORD bless you and keep you; the LORD make his face shine upon you and be gracious to you; the LORD turn his face toward you and give you peace."
—Numbers 6:24–26

We now come to the second blessing: the blessing of the Son. Through eternal ages the Son of God, in the fullness of time He became the Son of Man. He came to manifest, as well as to speak of, the Father's love. Time would fail us to enumerate the acts of typical service fulfilled in Him.

"The LORD make his face shine upon you." The face is perhaps the most wonderful part of the wonderful human body. Of all the faces that God has made no two are exactly alike, even when still. Though we occasionally meet those who bear a very close resemblance, intimate friends, who know the play of the countenance, never mistake. And why is this? Because God has so ordered it that the face shall reveal the character and feelings of the individual. And it is the purpose of God that the heart of Christ shall be revealed to His people. It is the will of God that "the light of the knowledge of the glory of God" should be revealed to us "in the face of Christ" (2 Cor. 4:6).

Where there is the shining of the face we know there is more than forgiveness, there is favor. "Restore us, O God Almighty; make your face shine upon us, that we may be saved" (Ps. 80:7). What a wonderful view of the light of His countenance the favored disciples must have had who were witnesses to His transfiguration! We are told His face did shine as the sun. To the proto-martyr Stephen the heavens were opened and the face of the Lord shone upon him, and when he saw Him he became so like Him that his dying utterances corresponded to those of his Lord on the cross. When Saul, likewise, saw the glory of the risen Savior, the vision at midday was of a light above the brightness of the sun; and the effect of that vision changed his whole life. And when the Lord makes the light of His countenance to shine upon any of His people there is a moral and progressive change into His likeness.

———*◊◊◊*———

Lord Jesus, it is the light of the knowledge of the glory of God that transforms my life. I ask You to shine into my heart with the light of Your face. It is my one desire to see You as You really are. Amen.

THE BLESSING OF THE SPIRIT

———

*"The LORD bless you and keep you; the LORD
make his face shine upon you and be
gracious to you; the LORD turn his face
toward you and give you peace."*
—Numbers 6:24–26

The blessing of the Spirit is essential to the completeness of the benediction. We are struck, however, with the similarity of this blessing to that which precedes it; nor is this similarity surprising, for, as the Son came to reveal the Father, so the Spirit has come to reveal the Son. Christ has a true Comforter, and the Holy Spirit is the other Comforter, sent by the Father in Christ's name, that He might abide with the Church forever. Christ is the indwelling Savior, the Holy Spirit the indwelling Comforter. On whomever Christ makes His face to shine, the Holy Spirit will surely lift up His countenance.

"And give you peace." Are we practically enjoying this blessing? Are we finding that when He makes quietness, none can make trouble? And if not, why not?

We shall never forget the blessing we received through the words, "Whoever drinks the water I give him will never thirst" (John 4:14). As we realized that Christ literally meant what He said—that "will" meant will, and "never" meant never, and "thirst" meant thirst—our heart overflowed with joy as we accepted the gift. Oh, the thirst with which we sat down, but oh, the joy with which we sprang from our seat, praising the Lord that the thirsting days were all past, and past forever! For, as our Lord continues, "Indeed, the water I give him will become in him a spring of water welling up to eternal life." Perhaps, however, we should draw attention to the words of Christ: "whoever drinks," not drank— once for all—but "drinks," that is, habitually. After promising that out of him "streams of living water will flow," it is added, "By this he meant the Spirit, whom those who believed in him were later to receive" (John 7:38–39). It is intended for all who believe—"and give you peace." Would that each reader would accept the gift *now.*

—————

Holy Spirit, You are the eternal spring of living water that I thirst for. Only You can make Jesus real to me. Fill me with Your peace and power. Amen.

BLESSED ADVERSITY

—⚬⚬⚬—

"The LORD gave and the LORD has taken away;
may the name of the LORD be praised."
—Job 1:21

All of God's dealings are full of blessing. He is good, and does good, good only, and continually. The believer who has taken the Lord as his Shepherd can assuredly say in the words of the psalmist, "Surely goodness and love will follow me all the days of my life" (Ps. 23:6). Hence we may be sure that days of adversity, as well as days of prosperity, are full of blessing. The believer does not need to wait until he sees the reason of God's afflictive dealings with him before he is satisfied; he *knows* that all things work together for good to them that love God (Rom. 8:28).

The history of Job should teach us many lessons of deep interest and profit. The veil is taken away from the unseen world, and we learn much of the power of our great adversary, but also of his powerlessness apart from the permission of God our Father.

Satan would very frequently harass the believer in times of sorrow and trial by leading him to think that God is angry with him. But our heavenly Father delights to trust a trustworthy child with trial. Take the case of Abraham: God so trusted him that He was not afraid to call upon His servant to offer up his well-beloved son. And in the case of Job, it was not Satan who challenged God about Job, but God who challenged the arch-enemy to find any flaw in Job's character. In each case grace triumphed, and in each case patience and fidelity were rewarded.

The reply of Satan is noteworthy. He *had* considered God's servant and evidently knew all about him. The arch-enemy had found all his own efforts ineffectual to harass and lead astray God's beloved servant. He had found a hedge around Job, and about his servants, and about his house, and about all that he had on every side. How blessed to dwell so protected.

Is there no analogous spiritual blessing to be enjoyed now? Thank God there is. Every believer may be as safely kept and as fully blessed.

Almighty God, help me to see that I dwell in the shadow of Your wings, and that I'm kept by Your power for a salvation that one day will be revealed for all to see. I praise You for the hedge of protection around my life. Keep me focused on You. Amen.

ALL-SUFFICIENCY

—*ᗡᑗᗡ*—

For the LORD God is a sun and shield; the LORD
bestows favor and honor; no good thing does he
withhold from those whose walk is blameless.
—Psalm 84:11

The Lord God is a Sun and Shield, and this
in the fullest conceivable sense. None of His
works can fully reveal the great Designer, the
Executor and Upholder; and the loftiest
thoughts and imaginations of the finite mind
can never rise up and comprehend the
Infinite. The natural sun is inconceivably
great, we cannot grasp its magnitude; it is
inconceivably glorious, we cannot bear to
gaze on one ray of its untempered light. And
yet it may be the very smallest of all the
countless suns that God has made! What of
the glorious Maker of them all!

The Lord God is a Sun. He is the Reality of
all that sun or suns suggest. My reader, is He
the Sun to you? And the Lord God is a Shield.
Dangers encompass us at every moment.
Within us and around us are dangers unseen

that at any moment might terminate our earthly career. Why do we live so safely then? Because the Lord God is a Shield. The world, the flesh, and the devil are very real; and unaided we have no power to keep or deliver ourselves from them. But the Lord God is a Shield. It is a small thing then to go to China, a very small additional risk to run, for there as here the Lord God is a Shield. To know and do His will—this is our safety and rest.

Sweet are His promises—grace will He give and glory. Grace all unmerited and free. And glory too—glory *now*, the glory of being His, of serving Him, and glory in the soul. No good thing will He withhold from those who walk uprightly. Ah, how often when we have been dissatisfied with the ways of God, we should have been dissatisfied with our own ways.

But sweet as God's promises are, the Promiser is greater and better. Hence if we had claimed all the promises, and had opened our mouths wide, He would still be able to do exceedingly above all we ask or think. He delights to do so.

―――∾∾∾―――

Lord God, a day doesn't go by where I don't fail to comprehend Your magnificance. Help me to bask in the sunshine of Your love today, and to glory in the safety of belonging to You. I open wide my heart that You might fill it. Amen.

DIVINE POSSESSION AND GOVERNMENT

———&&&———

*When Israel came out of Egypt, the house of Jacob
from a people of foreign tongue, Judah became
God's sanctuary, Israel his dominion. The sea looked
and fled, the Jordan turned back; the mountains
skipped like rams, the hills like lambs.*
—Psalm 114:1–4

Judah sadly failed to apprehend God's presence in their midst, and Israel proved both faithless and insubordinate through the entire ordeal. But all this did not annul the *fact* that Israel had a King, and that that King was a mighty One. Strange that man alone should resist His Maker. But blessed is the truth that His presence is not dependent upon our apprehension of it, nor His power to save necessarily limited by our lack of faith. "The sea looked and fled, the Jordan turned back."

But if this was the case, despite the sin and failure of the people, what would have been the blessing had faith been in constant exercise? Blessed, oh, blessed indeed, is he who yields his whole being to his Savior and his God, for His indwelling and governance.

Apart from this His indwelling and governance how truly helpless we are, and how often hopeless we become! But how changed all this becomes when it is no longer "I," but "Christ" who "lives in me!" Then, we do not cry to be delivered *out* of the body of this death, but the life that we live—though still *in* the flesh—we live in the faith (faithfulness) of the Son of God, who loved us and gave Himself for us.

We shall not find this new life a life without conflict. The world still remains the world; the flesh still remains the flesh; the devil still remains the devil. Escaped from Egypt, Egypt will pursue us; but whereas the Red Sea would prove an insuperable barrier to the carnal mind, if Christ is indwelling, the sea sees it and flees, and we begin to find that there is *no hindrance in the presence of our Master and King*. The proud waves of the sea, the swellings of Jordan overflowing its banks, own the presence of Him, who when on earth calmed the fears of the fishermen on the Sea of Galilee and said, "Peace, be still!" to the raging waves. Mountains of difficulties skip out of the way like rams, and the more numerous little hills in His presence became harmless as lambs.

—◦◦◦—

Father, the world, the flesh, and the devil never give up the battle. It is only Your presence in my life that overcomes the darkness. Make Your presence known today. Amen.

DIVINE POSSESSION AND GOVERNMENT

———

Why was it, O sea, that you fled, O Jordan,
that you turned back, you mountains, that you
skipped like rams, you hills, like lambs? Tremble,
O earth, at the presence of the Lord, at the
presence of the God of Jacob.
—Psalm 114:5–7

In the history of the bringing out of Israel from Egypt and into the promised land, the role of the wilderness figures in significantly, but we find no mention of it in this psalm—it disappears with the faithless generation who were buried in it. Why is this? Because in the life of faith there is no wilderness. The sea—the boundary on this side—sees our Master and flees; Jordan—the boundary on that side—in His presence is driven back. The wilderness is for unbelievers, who *will not* enter into rest.

We have been brought into a goodly land; the mountains and the little hills alike proved no barriers. In the presence of the Master, there remains no wilderness. Even those earthly blessings that are His own good gift He

often sees fit to remove. He has promised—
promised but not threatened: "'Once more I
will shake not only the earth but also the
heavens.' The words 'once more' indicate the
removing of what can be shaken—that is, cre-
ated things—so that what cannot be shaken
may remain" (Heb. 12:26–27). Perhaps sometimes we fail to realize how great a cause for
thankfulness we have, when a loving Father
removes some prop that can be shaken, on
which we were leaning all too fondly, instead
of resting alone on the Rock of Ages—a prop
that was to some extent eclipsing our view of
His Kingdom. Perhaps He saw that we were
too content to rest on our oars or trust a
mooring post that prevented us from drifting
with the current, but was incompatible with
our making progress up stream, and with that
arduous battling with the wild waters around
that was a needful training for future victories.

There is a day coming in which not only
will the sea flee and Jordan be turned back,
but heaven and earth will flee away at the
presence of the Lord, the God of Jacob. It is
with this Mighty One we have to do, not with
mountains and hills, rivers or seas. May we not
be content with *any* circumstances and *any*
surroundings, when He has said, "Never will I
leave you; never will I forsake you" (Heb. 13:5).

———⁓⁓⁓———

Lord, You alone are my helper; I will not be afraid.
What can man do to me? Shake the props out of my
life and strengthen me for Your service. Amen.

ABIDING IN CHRIST

———∾∿∾———

*"Remain in me, and I will remain in you.
No branch can bear fruit by itself; it must
remain in the vine. Neither can you bear
fruit unless you remain in me."*
—John 15:4

We need not enlarge upon the importance that Jesus gives to abiding in Him. If we do not abide in Him, it is not that we bear less fruit or inferior fruit, but apart from Him we can do *nothing.* It is either fruit and abiding, or no fruit at all, nothing but mere works. The distinction between fruit and works is important. Works do not show the character of the worker, but only his skill: a bad man may make a good chair. Works, it is true, may be good and useful, but they do not propagate themselves. Fruit, on the contrary, reveals the character of the fruit-bearer, and has its seed in itself—is productive.

What is the meaning of the words "Remain in me, and I will remain in you"? The two words, "I am," are the key to this chapter. The question is not what *you* are, not what *you* can do. "I am the true vine," and further, "my Father is the gardener." Jesus turns our thoughts away from self altogether, and practically says, "Believe in God, believe also in me."

"I am the vine." He is not just any part of the vine, but the whole vine. The vine is the whole tree—root, trunk, branches, twigs, leaves, flowers, fruit. Some of us, failing to see this, have read the passage as though it were written, "I am the root; you are the branches;" and we have said, "Ah! There is sap enough in the root, but how am I to get its riches into my poor, puny branch?" The branch gets nothing *out* of the vine, it enjoys all *in* the vine. So are we *in* Christ.

The little word "in" requires more than a passing notice. It is not in the sense of within, as when the less is contained within the greater. As used in the text, *in* implies *union with,* identification. The branch is vitally and organically one with the vine, as the eye or ear is *in* the body. And the word "remain" conveys the idea of rest rather than of labor or motion, of enjoyment attained, not of seeking and striving.

The twofold expression indicates a mutual indwelling. Recognize both truths, not sometimes, but at all times.

―――*ᴠᴠᴠ*―――

Jesus, I am happy to be joined to You like a branch in a vine. I rest in You. I draw my life and being from You. O may I bear fruit that brings honor to You. Amen.

HUMILITY

—∿∿∿—

Who, being in very nature God, did not consider
equality with God something to be grasped, but
made himself nothing, taking the very nature of a
servant, being made in human likeness.
—Philippians 2:6–7

For you know the grace of our Lord Jesus
Christ, that though he was rich, yet for your
sakes he became poor, so that you through his
poverty might become rich" (2 Cor. 8:9). "Your
attitude should be the same as that of Christ
Jesus" (Phil. 2:5).

Will anyone reflect on what the Son of
God gave up in leaving heaven's throne to be
cradled in a manger; who, having filled all
things and wielded omnipotence, became a
feeble infant and was wrapped in swaddling
clothes; who being the Beloved of the Father,
never unappreciated, never misunderstood,
and receiving the ceaseless adoration of the
hierarchies of heaven, became a despised
Nazarene, misunderstood by His most faithful
followers, suspected by those whom He came
to bless, neglected and rejected by those who

owed Him their very being, and whose salvation He had come to seek; and, finally, mocked and spit upon, crucified and slain, with thieves, bandits, and outlaws. Will you reflect on this and still hesitate to make the small sacrifices to which He calls you? Shall we be not prepared to give up not only these little things, but a thousand more for Christ? I believe it is your desire, through grace, not to count your life dear to yourself, but that you might finish your course with joy and the ministry that you received from the Lord Jesus.

Let there be no reservation; give yourself up wholly and fully to Him whose you are, and whom you wish to serve in this work, and then there can be no disappointment. But if you allow the question to arise, "Am I called to give this up?" or admit the thought, "I did not expect this or that inconvenience or sacrifice," then your service will cease to be that free and happy one that is most conducive to success. "God loves a cheerful giver" (2 Cor. 9:7).

———*◊◊◊*———

Beloved of the Father, I bow before You in awe of Your infinite sacrifice on my behalf. I yield my heart and soul completely to You. By Your grace may I know Your calling and complete it with joy. Amen.

GOD'S GUARDIAN CARE

—∞—

The LORD is my shepherd,
I shall not be in want.
—Psalm 23:1

It is the will of our Father that His children shall be absolutely without worry and carefulness. "Do not be anxious about anything" (Phil. 4:6) is as definite a command as "You shall not steal" (Exod. 20:15). To enable us, however, to carry out this command, we need to *know* the constancy of His solicitude who ever cares for us; and we need to make use of the directive:"In everything, by prayer and petition, with thanksgiving, present your requests to God" (Phil. 4:6).

The comfort of this blessed assurance is the happy portion of all the people of God; of our friends and supporters at home, equally with our toiling laborers abroad.

What a comfort it is to notice how largely the indicative mood is used in the Scriptures. In the present psalm, for instance, we find the subjunctive mood only in one clause of the fourth verse. All the definiteness and assurance we can desire are conveyed by positive affirmations in the indicative mood, and it is noteworthy that each encouragement is either conveyed in the present tense, or is based upon it: "The LORD *is* my shepherd, I *shall* not be in want."

It is comforting to remember that for the sake of His own Name, and of His own glory, as well as for the sake of His great love, the full supply of all our needs is guaranteed by our relationship to Him as our Shepherd. A lean, scraggy sheep with torn limbs and tattered fleece would be small credit to the shepherd's care; but unless we *will* wander from Him, and *will not* remain restfully under His protection, there is no fear of such ever being our lot.

"The LORD *is* my shepherd." He does not say *was*, or *may be*, or *will be*. "The LORD *is* my shepherd"—*is* on Sunday, *is* on Monday, and *is* through every day of the week; *is* in January, and *is* in December, and in every month of the year; *is* at home, and *is* in China; *is* in peace and *is* in war; in abundance and in need. Let us live in the joy of this truth.

—◦◦◦—

Good Shepherd, forgive me if I've wandered away from Your care, or if I've allowed a sense of distance to come into my relationship with You. Restore to me the joy of knowing that You are the Shepherd of my soul both now and forevermore. Amen.

GOD'S GUARANTEES

—⁓—

*"But seek first his kingdom and his
righteousness, and all these things will
be given to you as well."*
—Matthew 6:33

It is the position of our China Inland Mission
to invite the cooperation of fellow believers,
irrespective of denomination, who fully
believed in the inspiration of God's Word, and
were willing to prove their faith by going into
Inland China with only the guarantees they
carried within the covers of their pocket
Bibles. God had said, "But seek first his kingdom and his righteousness, and all these
things [food and clothing] will be given to
you as well." If anyone did not believe that
God spoke the truth, it would be better for him
not to go to China to propagate the faith. If he
did believe it, surely the promise sufficed.

Again: "No good thing does he withhold
from those whose walk is blameless" (Ps.
84:11). If anyone did not mean to walk
uprightly, he had better stay at home; if he did

mean to walk uprightly, he had all he needed in the shape of a guarantee fund. God owns all the gold and silver in the world, and the cattle on a thousand hills.

Money wrongly placed, and money given from wrong motives, are both to be greatly dreaded. We can afford to have as little as the Lord chooses to give, but we cannot afford to have unconsecrated money, or to have money placed in the wrong position. Far better to have no money at all, even to buy food with, for there are ravens in China that the Lord could send again with bread and fish. The Lord is always faithful; He tries the faith of His people, or rather their faithfulness. People say, "Lord, increase our faith." Did not the Lord rebuke His disciples for that prayer? He said, "You do not want a great faith, but faith in a great God. If your faith were as small as a grain of mustard seed, it would be enough to remove this mountain." We need a faith that rests on a great God, and that expects Him to keep His word and to do just what He has promised.

—◦◦◦◦—

Jesus, it is no secret to You how I handle my finances in relationship to Your kingdom work. May You always find me trusting in Your faithfulness rather than my personal means. Show me what it is in Your kingdom that you desire me to seek. Amen.

CONSIDERING THE WEAK

—◦◦◦—

Blessed is he who has regard for the weak; the
LORD delivers him in times of trouble.
—Psalm 41:1

This man's character so resembles that of
Christ that God considers him with favor. He
has beheld as in a glass the features of his
Lord, and like a glass reflects His character.
The heart of God goes out toward him, and
every needful good is bestowed. Is he in trouble, who has considered, and to the extent of
his ability helped, those in trouble? Will God
do less for him? No! The following verse
reads: "The LORD will protect him and pre-
serve his life; he will bless him in the land and
not surrender him to the desire of his foes."

But who is the one so blessed? Not the
one who cheaply relieves his own eyes of a
painful spectacle by a trifling alm, or relieves
himself of the importunity of a collector for
some benevolent cause. Not the one who qui-
ets his own conscience by gifts that really cost

no self-denial, and then dismisses the case of the poor and needy from his thoughts, complacently claiming the blessings promised to the charitable. As for those who seek fame and name by their gifts, we altogether dismiss their case from consideration. The blessing is pronounced on those who "regard" the poor, who turn their thoughts and attention toward the poor and needy, and who do what they can, at the cost of personal self-denial, to lessen the sum of human woe. Such *are* blessed indeed, and such *shall* be blessed: blessing is their inalienable portion.

Do not let us spiritualize the text so as to lose its obvious character. We Protestants are often in no small danger of doing this. How much of the precious time and strength of our Lord was spent in conferring temporal blessings on the poor, the afflicted, and the needy? Such ministrations, proceeding from right motives, cannot be lost. They are Godlike; they are Christlike.

I pen these lines in a Chinese boat, moored by a Chinese village. My heart is full; what shall I say? I implore you to consider the case of the poor, and may the Lord give you understanding.

—◦◦◦—

Jesus, I read the words and consider their meaning, but only Your Spirit can make my heart like Yours. Give me a heart for the poor, for the needy, for a lost world. Amen.

SPIRITUAL PREPARATION

—–⦿⦿⦿–—

*May your deeds be shown to your servants, your
splendor to their children. May the favor of the Lord
our God rest upon us; establish the work of our
hands for us—yes, establish the work of our hands.*
—Psalm 90:16–17.

The desire to be prosperous in our worldly
callings and in our spiritual enterprises is a
natural one, and there are few who are not
prepared to agree with Moses regarding his
last petition of Psalm 90. This petition is per-
fectly legitimate if kept in its proper place. It is
to be noted, however, that it is not found in
the first verse of the psalm, but in the last. If it
takes the same place in our hearts that it had
in the prayer of Moses, it will be a safe one for
us to offer.

The history of Moses is very instructive. He
was not a young man when he first attempted
to deliver Israel; nor, as men would say, was he
unequipped and untrained. Yet He lacked the
necessary spiritual preparation. He had not
come to the end of self, and therefore he
failed. He went forward "supposing." Humbled

and instructed by his failure, he did not again attempt their deliverance until it was pressed upon him by God Himself.

Mere deliverance from evil and from sorrow might lead to a self-satisfied life, devoid of knowledge of or interest in the great purposes of God. Hence Moses prayed, "May your deeds be shown to your servants, your splendor to their children."

The prayer is not less appropriate in our own day than it was in the time of Moses. And Moses prayed, "May the favor of the Lord our God rest upon us." Let it not merely be revealed to us, but let it be reflected by us, let it rest upon us. And when Moses came down from the mount the favor, or the beauty, of the Lord was upon him, so his prayer is that *all* the people of God may reflect the beauty of His character.

Shall we not be more concerned that the beauty of the Lord our God be upon us than that our work be established? Let this be the primary object. Then come in their proper place the petitions: "Establish the work of our hands for us—yes, establish the work of our hands."

———*∞∞*———

O Lord our God, my priorities in prayer are so often backward. Instruct me in Your ways, show me Your great deeds and the splendor of Your Son, and may Your favor and beauty rest upon me as I seek to glorify You in all I do. Amen.

PRINCE · AND · SAVIOR

———◦◊◦———

God exalted him to his own right hand as Prince
and Savior that he might give repentance
and forgiveness of sins to Israel.
—Acts 5:31

These words from Peter indicate the offices to which Christ is raised by God. Let us mark well the order; you must accept the Prince if you would receive the Savior. Many wish they were saved, and remain unconverted, because they do not yield themselves, their wills, their all to God. Many others are only half saved, because they do not accept the Prince for this life, and consequently have no Savior to deliver them effectively in the hour of temptation. They see their life pictured as they watch some little child trying to walk; it can creep, but when it tries to walk it stumbles and falls. So it is with kingless lives. Oh, it does not pay to refuse the King! As the prodigal starved and was clothed with rags while the Father's house had the best robe waiting and the fatted calf, so there is rest, there is peace and joy, there is fruitfulness and power *inside* the Kingdom.

Is it so with you, my reader? Do you prosper in all you undertake? Are all your prayers answered? Does each morning bring you no fear? Is each day a psalm, each night a thanksgiving, sometimes sung in the minor key—but still sung? Do those around you see the witness of the Kingdom in your life? Does He reign in your work as well as your wardrobe? Do your visitors feel impressed with the reality of the Kingdom? Or, are there many things, some things, perhaps only one little thing, about which you claim to decide for yourself? Remember that only *one such claim dethrones altogether* your Lord and Master, so far as lies in your power, no matter how trivial the matter is. It says, "I will not have this Man to reign over me." If you were living or meant to live in accordance with His will, you would be only too glad to let Him be King, and to take in all His fullness, as you gave Him all your weakness and failure. Is He King to you when He says, "Therefore go and make disciples of all nations" (Matt. 28:19)?

———∽∾∽———

Search my heart, O God, and take Your place as the absolute Lord of my life. Break down those things that prevent You from being my Prince as well as Savior. Amen.

SPIRITUAL SCIENCE

—◦◦◦—

For you know the grace of our Lord Jesus
Christ, that though he was rich, yet for your
sakes he became poor, so that you through
his poverty might become rich.
—2 Corinthians 8:9

There are clear conditions for success in one's spiritual life. Ignoring these, we may work hard, sow much seed, and reap little. Has not the failure of many of our efforts been due to our attempting to do God's work in man's way—yes, and sometimes even in the devil's way. Does this seem a startling question? I suggest that you read the account of the temptations of our Lord, after His baptism, and see what Satan's ways are (Matt. 4). Have they not *often* been used, unknowingly, to forward the work for God? Have not Christians at home and abroad often been induced to *begin* work, and perhaps still more often to *continue* work, by incentives of promised support and position? Would the same sums of money marked for God's work always be contributed if the plate were not passed, or if the donors' names were not published?

When the Lord of glory came to bring the highest blessing, He chose the lowest place, as that best adapted to accomplish His purpose. In like manner, *in order to enrich us,* poor bankrupts, He intelligently and cheerfully *emptied Himself* of all His riches, as neither needed nor suited to effect His purpose. We do well to remember that He was the *Wisdom* of God and the *Power* of God, and necessarily chose the *wisest* way and the *mightiest* way to effect His purpose. He could have become incarnate as a noble Roman, I suspect, and He would undoubtedly have gained disciples by it—but of what kind? Or He might have come into the family of a noble and wealthy Jew, but He did not—that was not God's way.

The Corinthian believers knew the grace of the Lord Jesus Christ, that though He was rich, yet for their sakes He became poor. Do we? Do we want to know it? Are we imitators of God if we make no costly sacrifices for the salvation of men? It is our Isaacs who are wanted for the altar, not our luxuries. Are we followers of Christ if we do not walk in love, as Christ also loved us and gave Himself up for us?

———

Holy Spirit, search my heart and reveal the truth of what You find. If there is anything or anyone in my life that You desire for the altar, help me to surrender now. Amen.

SPIRITUAL SCIENCE

———

*For you know the grace of our Lord Jesus
Christ, that though he was rich, yet for your
sakes he became poor, so that you through
his poverty might become rich.*
—2 Corinthians 8:9

There is a natural science of which wise
men avail themselves, and by which they
accomplish great results unheard of by our
forefathers. Our God is the God of nature as
well as of grace; and as He always acts in the
best way, so, in the same circumstances, He
always acts in the *same* way. The uniformity of
His mode of action in nature is seen and rec-
ognized by many who do not know the great
Actor. Such often prefer to speak of the constancy of the laws of nature rather than of the
uniformity of the operations of God. But if we
speak of the laws of nature, let us not misun-
derstand the expression. It is the law of a well-
regulated household that the door is opened
when the door bell is rung. It would be an
entire mistake, however, to suppose that this is
done by the law: it is done, no matter whether

directly or mediately, by the head of the household. So a sparrow "will [not] fall to the ground apart from the will of your Father" (Matt. 10:29).

We who know God, and are His children, do well to remind ourselves that is *our unchanging* God who makes the water on the fire to boil, and the steam in the engine to develop such expansive power; that it is He who acts uniformly in electricity, whether we avail ourselves of His power in the use of the light bulb or succumb to it in the fatal lightning bolt; and that it is *His uniform action* that we recognize as the law of gravitation.

No less constant and sovereign is He in the domain of grace: His sovereignty is never erratic or arbitrary. His method of action may be studied and largely discovered in spiritual things as in natural. Some of His laws are plainly revealed in His Word; others are exemplified in the actions recorded therein. And best of all, by the illumination of the Holy Spirit, God Himself may be known, and loved, and revered, through the study of His written Word; and He is especially seen in the face of Jesus Christ.

———

Heavenly Father, just as we depend on the natural laws in our daily lives, so we depend upon You as the unchanging God of grace. Your sovereign rule has opened the door of salvation to me, and I rejoice that nothing can shut that door. Amen.

SPIRITUAL SCIENCE

—◦◦◦—

*For you know the grace of our Lord Jesus
Christ, that though he was rich, yet for your
sakes he became poor, so that you through
his poverty might become rich.*
—2 Corinthians 8:9

The indispensable illumination of the Holy
Spirit is never denied to those who seek it and
are honestly desirous to have it *on God's own
terms.* Spiritual things can only be spiritually
discerned; but those who are spiritual have
no more difficulty in learning spiritual laws
(by which we mean God's uniform mode of
acting in the same circumstances in spiritual
things), than natural men have in learning natural laws. Actually, in spiritual things there is
less difficulty, for they are revealed more
clearly. Research into the works and ways of
God more readily shows us His modes of
action than research and observation do in
natural science. Some of the secrets of nature
can only be known by a few, but the secrets of
grace may be known by *all* the children of
God, if they are *willing* to be taught and are
obedient as they are taught.

As in natural things there are many mysteries beyond the knowledge of man, so also in spiritual things there are things not yet revealed, not intended to be known here and now. But just as by utilizing what may be known and is known in nature men achieve great results—as by electricity, steam and gas engines, etc.—so by utilizing what is revealed and may be known in spiritual things great results may be achieved. Ten thousand horses could not convey the loads from London to Glasgow in a week that are easily taken in half a day by rail; ten thousand couriers could not convey the tidings from London to Shanghai in months that can be flashed by telegraph in a few hours. And so in spiritual things no amount of labor and machinery will accomplish without spiritual power, what may easily be accomplished when we place ourselves in the current of God's will, and work by His direction, in His way.

—∞—

Holy Spirit, today I ask you to take spiritual truth and make it real in my life. May the secrets of grace be plain for me to see. I place myself in the current of Your will. Amen.

IN HIS LIKENESS

———⁕———

"Be perfect, therefore, as your
heavenly Father is perfect."
—Matthew 5:48

We are to be the salt of the earth and the light of the world, not to break one of the least of God's commandments, not to yield to anger, not to tolerate impure thoughts, not to give rash promises, and never to speak evil of others. The spirit of retaliation is not to be indulged in; a yieldedness of spirit is to characterize the child of the kingdom of God, and those who hate and despitefully use us are to be pitied, and loved, and prayed for.

In the little frictions of daily life, as well as in the more serious trials and persecutions to which the Christian is exposed, he is manifestly to be an imitator of his heavenly Father. Now, God's perfection is an absolute perfection, while ours, at best, is only relative. A needle may be a perfect needle, in every way adapted for its work, but it is not a microscopic object; under the magnifying power it becomes a rough, honeycombed poker. So we are not called to be perfect angels or in any respect divine, but we are to be perfect Christians, performing the privileged duties that are given to us.

Now our Father makes, *according to His perfection*, the least little things that He makes. The tiniest fly, the smallest animalcule, the dust of a butterfly's wing, however highly you may magnify them, are seen to be absolutely perfect. Should not the little things of daily life be as relatively perfect in the case of the believer as lesser creations of God are perfect as His work? Ought we not to glorify God in everything we do as Christians, and should it not be more than unconverted people can be expected to do? Ought we not be more thorough in our service, not simply doing well that which will be seen and noticed, but, as our Father makes many a flower to bloom unseen in the lonely desert, so to do all that we can do as under His eye, though no other eye ever takes note of it?

Holy Spirit, may Your presence be so real to me today that even in the smallest of things, may I do them from a perfect heart of love for the Father. If no one takes notice, I know that You will see it clearly. Work in me the perfection that makes Your heart glad. Amen.

THE PRINCE OF PEACE

—◦◦◦—

And he will be called Wonderful
Counselor, Mighty God, Everlasting
Father, Prince of Peace.
—Isaiah 9:6

One of the titles given to our Lord in the prophecies of Isaiah is "Wonderful Counselor"; and truly He is wonderful in counsel and excellent in working. By ways very different from those which we could devise or execute, He trains His people in their service, and thus He prepares them for the inheritance of the saints in light. Then, when they are prepared for it, when the last polish has been received and the last refinement has been gained, He takes away those whom we would rather retain to grace the Paradise above.

We do not know what He is preparing us for, and consequently we often do not and cannot understand many of His dealings. But we can do what is better—we can trust Him. Triumphant faith—not merely submission to the will of God, but exulting delight in it, even when most crushing to flesh and blood—can *now* sing in anticipation, as we shall all sing soon together, "Our Jesus has done all things well."

In the passage from Isaiah, the prophecy tells us that the government shall be upon the shoulders of the Wonderful Counselor, whose name is also called the Prince of Peace. And it continues, "Of the increase of his government and peace there will be no end" (Isa. 9:7). First, He is brought before us, then His government and its peace, unending peace. How often we lack the peace because of a lack of hearty acceptance of Him and acquiescence in and cooperation with His government.

And yet that government is no harsh or arbitrary one. The hand that holds the scepter is a pierced hand, and the shoulder on which it rests first bore for each one of us the heavy cross. Is it not safe to trust the government of One whose love has redeemed us at such a cost, and made us His own at the price of His blood?

———*જ્ઞજ્ઞ*———

You are both wonderful in counsel and excellent in working. I celebrate Your kingdom and rule as the Prince of Peace. May I learn to trust You more and cooperate with You when I don't understand. Amen.

TO THIS YOU WERE CALLED

———

*Who, being in very nature God, did not consider
equality with God something to be grasped, but
made himself nothing, taking the very nature of a
servant, being made in human likeness.*
—Philippians 2:6–7.

The Christian calling is as unintelligible and
as unattractive to unbelief as was the person
and work of our glorious Head. In the world's
judgment He had no beauty that they should
desire Him. It is possible to receive salvation
and eternal life through Christ, but with a very
imperfect appreciation of the nature, the priv-
ileges, and the responsibilities of our calling.

To what then are we called? *To do good, to
suffer for it, and to endure it patiently.* "A pretty
calling," cries Unbelief, and turns away in dis-
gust. "Sad, but true," responds many a true but
sad heart. "I thank You, O Father," says Strong
Faith, "for so it seemed good in Your sight." God
has not changed since the Holy Spirit
recorded the answer to the question given

above. Man has not changed, nor has the great enemy of souls changed.

Now none of the proceedings of God are arbitrary; all the acts and all the requirements of perfect wisdom and of perfect goodness must of necessity be wise and good. We are called when we so suffer to take it patiently—and more than patiently, thankfully and joyfully—because seen from a right point of view there is neither ground nor excuse for impatience, but on the contrary abundant cause for overflowing thanks and joy. The early Christians were neither fools nor madmen when they took joyfully the spoiling of their goods, exulting that their names were cast out as evil, and that they themselves were counted worthy to suffer.

To make the message intelligible, it must be *lived*. God says, in effect, "Go and live among these unconverted ones as My representative." Be really glad, and let them see that you are glad—at the cost of any personal wrong and suffering—to have the opportunity of making the grace of God intelligible. The greater the persecutions are, the greater the power of your testimony. Such testimony never was in vain.

———

Father, I desire to follow in the steps of Your Son, wherever He leads me. If that involves suffering for Your name's sake, help me to endure it with joy. Amen.

WINNING CHRIST

—–⁓⁓–—

What is more, I consider everything a loss compared to the surpassing greatness of knowing Christ Jesus my Lord, for whose sake I have lost all things. I consider them rubbish, that I may gain Christ.
—Philippians 3:8

Do we give sufficient attention to the theme of gaining Christ? It is our joy and privilege to know Him as God's unspeakable *gift,* but none knew this more fully than the apostle Paul. But was he satisfied with this knowledge? Or was Paul's soul-consuming desire, at all possible cost, to *gain* Christ; and thus to know Him, and the power of His resurrection, and the fellowship of His sufferings? O that Christ may be so known by us as a "living, bright reality" that our one desire—our one absorbing heart-passion may be that we personally *gain* Christ—that we personally know Him as the apostle longed to do.

What is meant by gaining Christ? The meaning of verb is to win by way of exchange. In the case of many a believer, it may be truthfully said that Christ has a large place in his heart, although he could not perhaps fully state that Christ *is* all, *in* all; much that is gain to him has not yet become loss that he might win Christ.

How may we win Christ? By gladly personally surrendering to His service that which naturally we should most value, and also by heartily acquiescing in each loss and each cross that a Father's love ordains.

We know that He does remove many of our sources of joy, and we know that He reveals Himself through the removal more fully than ever before. But it is a triumph of faith that brings great glory to God when, in the time of nature's sorrow, the whole soul of the believer rejoicingly accepts the Lord's dealings. When flesh and heart fail, when our fondest hopes and desires are crossed, when it is quite clear to us that it is His will, not ours, that is being done, and our hearts are enabled to rejoice in that will—then indeed do we *gain* Christ; and oh, what a winning is that!

—✦—

Dear Father, I want my one heart's passion to be like Paul's, to win You as the all in all of my life. Give me the eyes of faith to see Your great Son who is at work in my life. Give me grace to know Him and the power of His resurrection. Amen.